COUNTY MAYOR Duties:

Many of the duties and responsibilities of the county mayor are not specifically addressed in the Tennessee Code, but are a function of the fact that the county mayor is expected to provide leadership and direction to the county in most policy areas. This leadership duty of the county mayor is not easily defined. The county mayor should have a better picture of the total government operation than any other county official, and should also have the knowledge, information and leadership ability to steer the county in the direction most beneficial to the county's future. The county mayor is required to devote full time to the office of county mayor, except in counties where, by referendum, it has been determined that the work is insufficient to require a full time county mayor (5-6-105). However, this requirement does not necessarily mean that the county mayor cannot have another job or manage another business. It does mean that the county mayor should devote a normal working day's time to the office.

The county mayor is the accounting officer and chief financial officer of the county; he or she is charged with the care and custody of county property (unless the law specifically places the care and custody on another official, such as the chief administrative officer of the highway department for highway equipment) (5-6-108). While the county mayor is charged with care of county property, the county legislative body has the power to erect, control and dispose of county property (5-5-121), and the authority to levy taxes for this purpose (5-5-122).

The county mayor appoints members of county boards and committees and appoints department heads unless, as is frequently the case, the law specifically provides otherwise; these appointees are subject to confirmation by the county commission (5-6-106(c)). Unless there is a conflict of interest or other prohibition, the county mayor is free to appoint a member of the county legislative body in exercising the appointment power, although the appointee should not vote on the confirmation. Op. Tenn. Att'y Gen. U94-004 (January 4, 1994).

Approval of an appointee requires a commission majority; if the county commission does not approve an appointment, the county mayor must make another appointment that will also be required to be approved by the county commission. However, the county mayor has no control over the appointment of the internal committees of the county commission unless the county mayor serves as chair of the county commission.

The county mayor is authorized to employ secretarial and clerical assistants needed in the performance of the duties of the office of county mayor (5-6-116). The county commission fixes the salaries for such assistants, paid out of the general funds of the county (5-6-118).

While leadership is the most important responsibility of the county mayor, leadership alone is not enough to keep county government functioning properly. Smooth operation also requires that each county official perform statutory administrative duties in several different areas. As accounting officer and general agent of the county, the county mayor has the following specific responsibilities:

1. To have care and custody of all county property, except that in the custody of other officials.

2. To appoint and to fix compensation of an agent or attorney to take care of county property.

3. To control all books, papers and instruments of the office.

4. To audit all claims for money against the county.

5. To draw, without seal, all warrants on the county treasury.

6. To audit and settle accounts of the county trustee, and those of any other collector or receiver of county revenue, taxes or incomes, payable into the county treasury, and those of any persons entrusted to receive or expend any money of the county.

7. To require the above officers or persons to render and to settle their accounts as directed by law, or by the authority under which they act.

8. To enter in the warrant book, in order of issuance, the number, date, amount and name of the drawee of each warrant drawn upon the treasury.

9. To keep in a suitable book an account of the receipts and expenditures of the county, so as to show clearly the assets of the county, and the debts payable to and by it, balancing the account semiannually, and generally to superintend the financial concerns of the county.

10. To write a semiannual report to the county legislative body reflecting all money received and paid out, and a complete statement of the financial condition of the county; to settle the other accounts once every year (5-6-108).

As financial officer of the county, the county mayor has the following duties:

1. To draw a warrant on the county trustee for payment of any judgment recovered against, or debt due from, the county.

2. To reduce to writing the testimony of any witness examined by the mayor concerning any settlement and file the same.

3. To examine minutely and settle the accounts of county officers, referring to the records, documents, dockets and papers in the office to verify each item.

4. To report the settlement to the county legislative body, under an oath stating "that the county executive believes that the same contains a true schedule of the revenue collected by each officer, and which the county mayor is bound by law to pay to the county trustee."

5. To make duplicates of the settlements with the clerks of the circuit, chancery and appellate courts, to deliver one duplicate to the county clerk, and to file the others
in each clerk's office.

6. To make, from the list furnished him or her by the tax assessor, an enumeration of the persons engaged in occupations which are deemed privileges and subject to a privilege tax, which must be forwarded to the state department of revenue, with his or her official signature and seal, and to report the list to the county legislative body at its July term, following the assessment (5-6-110).

Powers. To carry out the responsibilities listed above, the county mayor has the following powers:

1. If there is no county attorney, to employ and/or retain counsel to advise the mayor and the members of the county legislative body as to their legal rights as members, to prepare resolutions for passage by the body, and to represent the county in suits brought by or against the county, except suits by the county to collect delinquent taxes. The attorney is entitled to a reasonable fee for his or her services

and/or retention to be fixed by a majority vote of the members of the county legislative body at a regular session, to be paid out of the county general fund.

2. To require clerks of courts to produce all records, documents and papers in their offices relative to county revenue collected by that officer.

3. To call or summon all witnesses having any knowledge relating to the county revenue.

4. To demand of each clerk an account, on oath, of all moneys collected for the use of the county, setting forth each separate item, from whom, and at what time received, and the source from which it was derived.

5. To call the collectors of the county tax, at the time prescribed by law, for the purpose of making a final settlement for the year past.

6. To call the county trustee to a settlement when required by law, or by the court.

7. To procure, at the county's expense, a well-bound book, and therein cause to be entered, on the left-hand pages, two regular accounts, one against the collectors of taxes and revenue, the other against the county trustee, stating the amount of the taxes for which the collectors are accountable, and each item with which each of the officers is chargeable, in behalf of the county, expressing the manner in which it became due and owing, or by whom paid. And, on the right-hand page, opposite the debits, the county mayor shall cause to be entered such item or credit to which either of the officers is entitled, plainly showing the amount thereof and to whom paid.

8. To transfer the balance, if any, either for or against the county, to their respective accounts to be opened for the ensuing year, so that the county executive may be enabled, when required by the county legislative body, plainly to show the state and condition of the county treasury, and in what manner the moneys thereof have been disbursed.

9. To demand of the county clerk a list of the amount of taxes put into the hands of the collector, and due and owing for that year, together with sufficient vouchers, showing the amount of moneys paid to the trustee, as required by law, for fines and forfeitures, and the amount of all appropriations made for the year by the county legislative body, with all necessary documents and vouchers showing any

receipts and disbursements of county money (5-6-112).

10. To act for the county clerk when the clerk cannot perform any official act because of interest or relationship (5-6-114).

County mayors, as well as former county mayors and county executives, may perform marriages (36-3-301).

These statutory powers and responsibilities are only a very few of the day-to-day duties performed by the county mayor. While these duties provide the framework for the county mayor's administrative functions, the details of the county mayor's responsibilities are spread throughout the laws concerning county government.

PERRY COUNTY, IT IS TIME TO MOVE FORWARD.

Ladies and gentlemen my name is Kevin Tinin. I am the son of the late Ko Tinin and Cheryl Tinin. I am a lifelong Perry County resident (Roans Creek and Sugar Hill) My wife Marsha and I are the parents of Christian and Connor. I am a school teacher at our PCHS and a Deacon at First Baptist Lobelville. I have also worked for the state of Tennessee as a Court Liaison. I have a Bachelor's in Education from The University of Tennessee as well as a Master's in Education in Leadership from Bethel, and I hold an administrator's license. I am also your Republican nominee for the position of County Mayor.

A wise man once told me, "Kids can live in Perry County or they can have a career."

If you allow me the privilege to work for your family as your mayor, I give you my word that I will work with all elected officials to help grow Perry County as a place that is known not just for our nature but as a place where our children do have employment opportunities once they have finished not just high school, but college. Our kids are the future of our Perry County. School safety must be a top priority. I cannot do this by myself. I need you. I will be visiting you between now and August.

As a taxpayer, I'll say I do not envision any situation where any increase is a good idea. All of us have to come together to work on tomorrow's solutions with today's resources.

I've professionally prepared children for the future for 19 years. It is time to prepare the future for them. If you believe as I do, on August 2nd, vote Tinin. Thank you for your support and consideration.

PRINCIPLES

Here are seven principles and issues important to me as a lifelong Perry County resident that I intend to focus on as your mayor:

1. **We (elected officials) must be committed to keeping taxes low.**

2. **We need to continue to focus on quality education and safety of our children.**

3. **We must continue to attract new jobs to our county.**

4. **We must work with our local and state law enforcement officers to continue to create a safer, drug-free Perry County.**

5. **All elected officials need to be fully transparent.**

6. **We need to continue to work with our Road Superintendent on our roads and infrastructure.**

7. **We need to focus on a fresh outlook on limited government.**

I want to be your mayor. Your vote matters. I cannot do it without you. The election is on August 2, 2018. I present a few stories from campaigning, economic strategies, and a plan of action that focuses not just on our natural resources, but also industry.

Respectfully,

Kevin Tinin

ECONOMIC STRATEGY

It is easy to say we can just click online for help from the Economic Development Administration. That is the starting point. There are multi-agency initiatives and other programs, but we cannot fully rely on big government to help us. The first principle to grasp is that solving economic problems is not a short-range project. Quick fixes and buzzword projects will not work.

So here's my strategic plan to attempt improvement:

1. Form a committee-but not just any committee. It needs to be small key group of community members. These members should be stakeholders in the community and people who are directly affected by the economy. Members of our committee should be there for the long run. A real problem with most groups is that they want to organize like a service club with annual elections and rotating members. It is better to look at this group as being there for the long run with gradual changes in leadership and members. The service club approach results in leaders trying to get short term programs in during the year they are the chairperson so that they look successful.

2. No problem stands alone. It is not just that we as a county don't have jobs. A lack of jobs is the symptom of other economic factors that are preventing business growth in the area. They are always interrelated to other problems. We will need to take into consideration all factors of a community including infrastructure, work force, education level, available industrial and business sites, competition, political situation, life style, and so forth.

3. Our Committee will prepare a list of all economic development resources: Every state has a myriad of economic development agencies. Most counties and regions have economic development organizations of some sort. It has become almost mandatory in order to receive a Federal or State grant that some element of economic development is being done. On top of all this, there are hundreds of consulting groups, both non-profit and for profit. Universities, Colleges and Jr. Colleges usually have some program that is related to economic development. Our goal is not to list these for you but to have you search them out. Start at the state level and work down. You will also need to contact Federal level help such as the Department of Agriculture's Rural Development Agency and the Economic Development Agency (EDA). There are others such as housing related agencies.

4. Our committee will contact as many of these organizations personally as we can and build a database of what services are available to you. Go through the claims and discover what concrete services they can do for Perry County. Most organizations involved in economic development are not paid for results; they are paid for programs. Programs earn grants, which cover the overhead. The results of the programs are hidden behind the smoke and mirrors or buzz words like "planning". Get down to the real deliverables that PC can use. Planning may well be one of the deliverables, but you will need others.

5.   Concentrate on what we can change.

6.   The Industrial Park in Lobelville is a prospective opportunity for growth in for not just Lobelville but the entire county. The sewer lines in regards to the Industrial Park need to be industry certified so that potential businesses can be enticed to build and bring industry. I do know that Linden and Lobelville mayors are indeed working on this. With this in mind, the commissioners and all mayors need to be united and transparent when meeting with the Industrial Board. Each side must know what the other side is doing.

7.   We need to continue to work on the infrastructure of our airport. This is a key to literally bringing in company CEO's.

DO THE JOB

My Daddy Ko Tinin was afraid when he became the manager of General Products in the 1992. I watched him be angry and afraid when he began the learning process of running the store, ordering inventory, managing employees, just every aspect of the job because he had never had to be that person.

When he relaxed, he started focusing not so much on the anger and the fear of being the boss, but the customers. He told me the best way to run the business was to run it for the people. Everything else, the stress, the inventory, the daily issues all work themselves out when you simply, "Do your job."

"If we all do our jobs, the workload while heavy, will be easier to carry."

DAY ONE

Today was a very successful day meeting new faces, laughing with kinfolks, speaking with folks about life, church, John Cena actually, the election-registering new voters and even praying with a gentleman.

So many people know me, know the man I am not because of anything I've done, but because of my Daddy, Ko. It was a real emotional day with so many of you speaking so fondly of him and my mom Cheryl.

Even though, it was just Connor and I campaigning from 8 AM to 6 PM, it was like my Dad was there too because all you knew him and spoke so highly of him. Thank you all.

USING OUR RESOURCES

I personally would like to see our county with our access to both the Tennessee and the Buffalo become a premier fishing and recreation destination. As a county, we need to utilize our natural resources to maximize our quality of life.

1. TWRA BOAT RAMPS
    I believe there are only a few TWRA boat ramps in our county. We need to work towards a Perry County where there are multiple TWRA ramps. This can be accomplished by your elected officials working with the TWRA. This is Other than those two; the only other access points are our local canoe rentals. The Buffalo in my view is the most under-utilized resource we have.
2. Mousetail Landing State Park has 1,247-acres. Again, our elected officials need to work together to get cabins put in there. Families love camping. Fishing, canoeing, and kayaking are perfect fits to increase growth in Perry County. Our local businesses will benefit from the increased tourism.
3. Other opportunities are at Mousetail as well. While on the campaign trail, I have learned that many people come to use the terrain at Mousetail to prepare for the Appalachian trails. Our

elected officials need to contract with TVA to use our inmates-the Trustees to construct and possible new trails to increase tourism.

THE HARD JOB

I spoke to the mayor of one of the largest up and coming cities in Tennessee today. He has had experience in multi-million dollar industry and he explained that being mayor was hands down the hardest job he had ever undertaken.

Preparation is the key.

He told me homework was needed to be done. The mayor must be a step ahead of every meeting meaning that the mayor must be essentially in the loop on everything financial. He further suggested that a successful mayor's office have a strong finance director. It was advised that the mayor must have a good working relationship with all elected officials.

When a politician campaigns to a voter, he is selling a belief that he is the one that said voter has to support. While that is true, the focus of the election should never be on the candidate. It should be on the citizen. The care of all citizens is the reason why anyone should want a public office. It is to serve the citizens. NO more, no less.

Destination Perry County

Part of what makes Perry County so great is we have a unique charm. Most people in Tennessee exhibit hospitality, but we here in PC do it better. I know some folks might be afraid that if we get too big we might lose some of the down-home charm. I don't think that is the case. As I wrote earlier about trying to make Perry County a destination based on our access to our rivers and our nature, why not focus as well on other elements of our county for tourism. This is where the Perry County Chamber of Commerce comes into play.

1. Look for visitors who are already coming to your region and determine what is attracting them. (We know the rivers, and our festivals, so as I wrote earlier, let us increase the access to the rivers and let us consider more festivals. More on that below.)

2. Identify what the community can do to gain more benefit from these visitors. It can be improving signage, providing more community information at places or businesses these people are already frequenting, or looking at services these visitors need that it would be easy to provide.

3. Look at our assets. In 2018, the Blooming Arts' Festival brought in 159 vendors. We need to do in Lobelville what Linden has accomplished. We are six voting districts, but one Perry County. I know Lobelville has had celebrations in the past. We need to continue this. Also, our wonderful Music on Main Street is a wonderful way to rock and roll family time in the summer. Why not see how we can make them not better because they are great but maybe bigger.

4. When a county is clear about what we have and know what we would like, it's time to ask for help from regional and state tourism offices. So, here's the additional concrete plan: Contact the Tennessee Department of Tourist Development AND Joanne Steele, President of Rural Tourism Marketing Group. Joanne assists small towns and their businesses in the development and marketing their tourism industry.

Here's one final thought on this. Linden had a theater in the past. Lexington has the Princess Theater which is a lovely, family-owned business that does well despite having bigger theater chains just thirty minutes away in Jackson. I have many wonderful memories like most of you of going to the Waverly theater and the Drive-In. Would it not be just amazing if somehow, some way, someday Perry County had a theater again?

YOU MATTER

2,830 Perry County citizens voted in the 2016 presidential election. There are close to 5000 registered voters.

A lot of people in the past have said, "I don't think my vote counts."

I said then and say now, "Your vote counts. It matters."

Elected officials are in charge ONLY because citizens' votes allow them to be.

"IT IS TIME TO MOVE FORWARD, PERRY COUNTY."

Lessons From The Campaign Trail

It's time to move forward. It's not just words but it is a single action centered on all of you, all of us, citizens moving Perry County forward so new opportunities blossom. The following areas are of need and improvement brought up by you the citizen:

A. Sanitation

B. Ambulance service

C. Tourism

D. Industry

Sanitation is at top of list. Getting garbage pick-up, sanitation centers, and recycling caught up with the 21st century are words spoken by concerned citizens.

The ambulance service. Getting newer vehicles with less wear as well as more up to date technologically to benefit citizens as well as employees are other points many have brought up.

Tourism grants to develop natural area in order to promote tourism as well as offer our citizens additional access to natural areas for family use are often thought about.

Now here is the one area where everyone agrees. We need more industry. So, we need to get the industrial park ready to move into the future of bringing jobs to county. This is imperative because wishing for and inviting potential businesses without making the appropriate arrangements i.e., land preparation is not leading the way for Perry County.

Drugs and Poverty

Talk Poverty.org reports Tennessee's population as 6,489,032 but the number in poverty is: 1,023,177. From 2009-2013, Perry County's citizens living below the poverty level was 21.1 %. Individuals below poverty level
28.6%

Source: 2012-2016 American Community Survey 5-Year Estimates

According to Tn.gov, about half (54%) of individuals dependent on opioids live in poverty.

How can we help folks addicted to drugs?

TDMHSAS funds substance abuse treatment at licensed alcohol and drug treatment facilities for individuals who are over 12 years old and are indigent with incomes less than 133% of the Federal Poverty Level with no insurance or limited insurance. TennCare provides substance abuse treatment services to Medicaid enrollees with a substance use diagnosis. There's more on this under the Q and A section.

How can opioid misuse be prevented?

Educate prescribers about Tennessee's Chronic Pain Guidelines.

Educate individuals about:

- The risk of misusing opioids
- The dangers of sharing medications with others
- Proper disposal of unused medications
- Work with others to help communities become drug free
- Involve faith communities

Questions and Answers

Would you ever consider raising taxes?

The commissioners are the ones who vote to raise taxes. As a taxpayer, I do not envision any situation where any increase is a good idea. All of us have to come together to work on tomorrow's solutions with today's resources. Perhaps the best thing to do is look for waste and areas where spending can be maximized.

What is the biggest challenge our county faces?

At first, the quick answer would be jobs, but I will say drugs. I understand that not everyone desires a factory job, but jobs are available in both Lobelville and Linden. What I understand to be true is that many folks do not work because of the inability to pass a drug test. Just recently, a few of our local churches met to try to see what more they as bodies of faith can do to help individuals and families. The war on drugs has been ongoing for years. We have to come together as one Perry County for our children's futures.

Tennessee borders eight other states and its highways crisscross four major cities in addition to traversing each of the borders. So clearly Tennessee is a transshipment state. It also is a consumer state, but not a source area for any drug except marijuana.

Compared to other states

- **Illicit drugs overall** – average for those 18 and older
- **Pharmaceuticals** – average for those 18 and older
- **Marijuana** – average for those 26 and older, moderately low for those 18-25
- **Cocaine** – moderately low for those 26 and older, low for those 18-25
- **Alcohol** – low for those 18 and older

Source: SAMHSA's most recent National Survey on Drug Use and Health, based on 2008-2009 annual averages. SAMHSA is the Substance Abuse & Mental Health Services Administration, part of the U.S. Department of Health and Human Services.

SAMHSA's National Helpline, 1-800-662-HELP (4357), (also known as the Treatment Referral Routing Service) or TTY: 1-800-487-4889 is a confidential, free, 24-hour-a-day, 365-day-a-year, information service, in English and Spanish, for individuals and family members facing mental and/or substance use disorders. This service provides referrals to local treatment facilities, support groups, and community-based organizations. Callers can also order free publications and other information.

How will you hit the ground running? Describe your first 100 days.

1. Form a committee-but not just any committee. It needs to be small key group of community members. These members should be stakeholders in the community and people who are directly affected by the economy. Members of our committee should be there for the long run. A real problem with most groups is that they want to organize like a service club with annual elections and rotating members. It is better to look at this group as being there for the long run with gradual changes in leadership and members. The service club approach results in leaders trying to get short term programs in during the year they are the chairperson so that they look successful. We will need to take into consideration all factors of a community including infrastructure, work force, education level, available industrial and business sites, competition, political situation, life style, and so forth.

2. **Our Committee will prepare a list of all economic development resources**: Every state has a myriad of economic development agencies. Most counties and regions have economic development organizations of some sort. It has become almost mandatory in order to receive a Federal or State grant that some element of economic development is being done. On top of all this, there are hundreds of consulting groups, both non-profit and for profit. Universities, Colleges and Jr. Colleges usually have some program that is related to economic development. Our goal is not to list these for you but to have you search them out. Start at the state level and work down. You will also need to contact Federal level help such as the Department of Agriculture's Rural Development Agency

and the Economic Development Agency (EDA). There are others such as housing related agencies.

3. Our committee will contact as many of these organizations personally as we can and build a database of what services are available to you. Go through the claims and discover what concrete services they can do for Perry County. Most organizations involved in economic development are not paid for results; they are paid for programs. Programs earn grants, which cover the overhead. The results of the programs are hidden behind the smoke and mirrors or buzz words like "planning". Get down to the real deliverables that PC can use. Planning may well be one of the deliverables, but you will need others.

4. The Industrial Board should be actively looking and meeting monthly to come up with new plans, ideas, and grants.

5. Perry County's elected officials need to continue to work with SCHRA AND AS MANY OTHER STATE OFFICIALS to continue to serve ALL CITIZENS.

6. All county offices should work toward correcting errors listed by the state's annual report.

7. We need to continue to use sound business practices, expand our services, and work to keep property taxes from rising.

8. We should continue to implement new technologies to improve efficiency and reduce operating costs.

"All of us have to come together to work on tomorrow's solutions with today's resources."

Perry County was founded November 14, 1819. On August 2, 2018 your vote decides our future.

Kevin Tinin
FOR COUNTY MAYOR

I've professionally prepared children for the future for 19 years. It is time to prepare the future for them.

Bachelor's in Education from The University of Tennessee
Master's in Education in Leadership
+an administrator's license